W9-DFV-089

DIGITAL CAREER BUILDING™

CAREER BUILDING THROUGH

ALTERNATE REALITY GAMING

MEG SWAINE

ROSEN
PUBLISHING®

GRAND ISLAND PUBLIC LIBRARY
New York

For Brent. Geeks need love too. :)

Published in 2008 by The Rosen Publishing Group, Inc.
29 East 21st Street, New York, NY 10010

Copyright © 2008 by The Rosen Publishing Group, Inc.

First Edition

Library of Congress Cataloging-in-Publication Data

Swaine, Meg.
Alternate reality gaming / Meg Swaine. — 1st ed.
    p. cm. — (Digital career building)
[Title with series title added] Digital career building through alternate reality gaming
ISBN-13: 978-1-4042-1357-9 (library binding)
1. Alternate reality games—Design—Vocational guidance. I. Title.
II. Title: Digital career building through alternate reality gaming.
GV1469.7.S93 2008
793.93—dc22

                                                        2007032597

Manufactured in China

11 08

CONTENTS

CHAPTER ONE

DEFINING THE GENRE

Fans logging on to the newly created promotional Web site for the upcoming film *The Dark Knight* in May 2007 found they could click through to another Web site, called IbelieveinHarveyDent.com. It contained a campaign poster for the *Batman* character Harvey Dent, set to appear in the next movie, played by actor Aaron Eckhart.

This in itself seemed like standard promotional fare, until employees at a comic book store started finding playing cards scattered along their floors, all sinisterly written on and stamped with the URL Ibelieveinharveydenttoo.com. The site that the URL led to looked much like the other one, but with one grave exception—it had been maniacally defaced in red paint.

The Web site IbelieveinHarveyDent.com is a popular alternate reality game promoting the upcoming Batman film, *The Dark Night.*

The alternate reality game for the upcoming film *The Dark Knight* doesn't just advertise the film; it also doles out tantalizing bits of the story and even involves the players themselves in it.

There was a field where visitors could enter their e-mail and receive the message "Check your e-mail now." The e-mail they received contained coordinates that, when entered, deleted a pixel from the picture. After enough pixels were deleted, a picture underneath was revealed— a creepy photo of Heath Ledger as the Joker in the upcoming Batman film, *The Dark Knight*.

The page was later replaced with a black page with the words "Page not found" in red letters. However, high-lighting the background revealed black-on-black text, which appeared to be only a series of "Ha's," with other letters scattered throughout that spelled out the ominous message "See you in December."

This intriguing online puzzle is yet another in the expanding genre known as alternate reality gaming (ARG), a nonlinear, puzzle-based form of interactive storytelling and play that uses the real world and the Internet to lead players to piece together clues using their own knowledge. The payoff can be anything from a large cash prize to simply finding out more about an upcoming film. But in the end, the drive to solve clues and discover where the rabbit hole leads is its own reward. This mixing of reality and fiction creates a suspension of disbelief that makes these stories all the more engaging.

You may be aware of past examples of alternate reality gaming, such as ilovebees.com (a *Halo 2* promotion) or the promotion of Nine Inch Nails' recent album, *Year Zero*. The *Year Zero* ARG started simply with mysterious flash drives being left in bathrooms at concerts, containing brand-new NIN tracks and clues that led them online.

This kind of wild goose chase is generally run in real time and requires a whole team of developers (known as puppet masters in the ARG world) who do not give hints and do not interact with the players, as themselves, until the game is finished. ARGs are usually not announced by the companies that fund them or make them, but the developers often design a series of obvious entry points or "rabbit holes" to draw people in.

A lot of work goes into designing the puzzles and acting the parts of the fictional characters, but the most work, by far, is keeping up with the player communities. It requires wits and good storytelling skills. Anybody with these two things and a good complement of digital know-how can help design an alternate reality game.

The Birth of a Genre: A Brief History

Alternate reality games, unsurprisingly, have not been around for long—after all, they rely heavily on the Internet! The very first ARG, *The Beast*, did not appear until 2001, a promotion for the film *Artificial Intelligence: AI*. But there are some other forms of storytelling that, in the past, have blurred the line between reality and fiction.

In 1988 and 1989, AOL (then Quantum) had an online story called the "Quantum Link Serial," which used chat, e-mail, and traditional storytelling. But the real twist was that readers could write in and suggest ways in which they could be integrated into the story. Each week, a handful of readers were chosen and given "cameos" in the story itself. The writer, Tracy Reed, adapted the story to the input of the readers, thereby making them contributors to it. Within three months, it was the highest-rated text segment of AOL. The "Quantum Link Serial" was included in the monthly subscription price.

The concept was resurrected in 1997, in *The Spot* by Scott Zakarin, which also used photos and videos, and was ad-supported instead.

In 1999, Nokia started running what is sometimes considered to be an alternate reality game called *The Nokia Ultimate Connection Game*, which was a story that took place across phone calls, magazines, and TV advertisements. The first Nokia game was run in the Netherlands but later branched out into other countries. Unlike later ARGs, the Nokia game was more competitive than collaborative (it was mostly single-player), and it was announced, rather than started in secret.

ALTERNATE REALITY GAMING

MISSING

Heather Donahue	Joshua Leonard	Michael Williams
Age: 22 Height: 5'6" Weight: 127lb	Age: 23 Height: 5'10" Weight: 152lb	Age: 24 Height: 5'8" Weight: 169lb
Eyes: hazel Hair: brown	Eyes: blue Hair: blonde	Eyes: brown Hair: brown

Last seen camping in the Black Hills Forrest area, near Burkitsville.

The Blair Witch Project took the horror film genre to a new level by continuing the story outside of the film itself.

In 1999, *The Blair Witch Project* by Haxan Films, an eerie horror flick seemingly recorded on a simple camcorder, was released. It was about three film students who get lost in the woods. Story material outside of the film itself was produced to make people wonder if it was real or not, carrying the suspension of disbelief even farther. "Missing Persons" posters were put up, and a documentary about the disappearance of the students was aired on the Sci-Fi channel, which examined the "evidence." Photos of the tapes that were found and scans of one of the student's journal also appeared on the Web site with "archival footage" on the history of fictional Burkittsville and the Blair settlement. This story material was so convincing that many people visited the real town of Burkittsville and inundated the county sheriff's office with questions about the supposedly missing film students.

None of it was meant as a deliberate hoax—there were plenty of obvious clues that the film was fictional. However, it was so enthralling and "real" that fans of the movie enjoyed immersing themselves in it. Ironically, people at Haxan Films later went on to help create the alternate reality game *The Art of the Heist*, which promoted the new Audi car. Their promotional experiment with *The Blair Witch Project* gave them new ideas about how they could attract people to more than just movies.

You may have noticed that other types of games and activities you participate in have similar "immersive" elements. For instance, have you ever organized an "Evening of Murder," a mystery game where guests at a party take on roles in a murder mystery and try to determine the murderer? This is the type of game that takes place in ordinary settings, under ordinary circumstances, much like an ARG.

Similarly, role-playing games such as *Dungeons and Dragons* or *Vampire* have one person, called the game master (GM), who controls the hypothetical setting and nonplayer characters. The players portray their own characters, who generally must complete a quest or enter hypothetical combat.

In live-action role-playing games, people act out these scenarios. Participants dress and act as their chosen characters, with specific rules and guidelines to the game's actions and combat, within a closed setting or convention.

ALTERNATE REALITY GAMING

Alternate reality gaming has roots in the genre of role-playing games, which rely just as much on quick thinking and storytelling.

This sort of game play is similar to performance art or improvisation.

Role-playing games are similar to ARGs in the respect that they take place in real time, and the players' actions determine what direction the story is going in. It is often up to the GM to adapt the story as it develops. After all, it's hard to predict what the players are going to do!

Alternate reality gaming combines these types of immersive story elements and real-time interaction usually in an online setting, and sometimes even more.

The Beast and *Majestic*

Two of the first definitive ARGs were developed almost simultaneously, by two different companies. A project nicknamed *The Beast* was created by Microsoft developers for the movie *Artificial Intelligence: AI*. Majestic, an interactive, multiplatform story, was developed by Electronic Arts.

In early 2001, during the promotion of the movie *Artificial Intelligence: AI*, strange references to a "sentient machine therapist" began to crop up on movie posters and trailers. There was also an encoded phone number, which, once called, started a series of clues that unraveled a murder mystery online. The game was nicknamed *The Beast* by the developers when they found there were 666 pieces to it. It played out as a murder mystery across multiple media, such as e-mail messages, faxes, fake ads, and voice mail, using a variety of puzzles and challenges. The story expanded the fictional world within the film. Players interacted with characters in the story; some even attended an anti-robot protest rally in real life. The company hired science fiction writer Sean Stewart to write the story. The game was amazingly successful, attracting three million players. An online community immediately sprung up around the game. Members called themselves "the Cloudmakers," after the name of a boat mentioned in the game. This community became instrumental in shaping and unfolding the story as it happened. The tagline "This is not a game" quickly became a mantra for alternate reality gaming.

Electronic Arts' *Majestic*, which launched the same year, did not fare as well. It was similar in nature to *The Beast* but ran into some major problems. First of all, *Majestic* was largely meant to be played individually and therefore had less teamwork appeal. Secondly, it was subscription based—the first "episode" was free,

Actors Ashley Scott and Jude Law in *Artificial Intelligence: AI*, a movie that established alternate reality gaming as a new venue for promoting films.

 Sean Stewart (www.seanstewart.org) has taken his highly skilled writing and used it to pioneer the world of ARGs with his work on *The Beast*.

but there was a fee for each following episode. Approximately 100,000 people signed up for the free pilot, but only about 10,000 to 15,000 subscribed to later episodes. *Majestic* was also unlucky enough to have a plot that centered on government conspiracy, a story theme that was considered ill timed by the fall of 2001. *Majestic* was cancelled before it was completed, due to lack of interest.

These two initial games represented the beginning of a trend that is only now really finding its way into mainstream media. Now that you have some idea of where alternate reality games started, you can begin to consider what kinds of things you can do with them

·ARGNet

ARGNet is the definitive resource for news and other up-to-date information on alternate reality gaming. Started in 2002, it covers ARGs that are currently running, contains useful links, and even has a regular podcast of ARG news. There's also a chat room for live discussion, and the site offers vital info for those new to the alternate reality gaming universe. By subscribing to the podcast or the e-mail list, you can keep up on what new games are starting and what else is happening in the world of alternate reality gaming. Check it out at http://www.argn.com.

creatively, either by learning how to design them yourself or by putting your well-earned skills from playing them to good use in your future career. Can you create a trail of hidden clues that lead to a story? Or maybe you can put your group problem-solving skills to work in a real-life situation. ARGs have the potential to train the next generation of Web detectives.

CHAPTER TWO

ARGS AS AN INDUSTRY

It's easy to see that alternate reality gaming is on the rise. *The Beast* in 2001 attracted over three million players from all over the world and found coverage in mainstream media, such as *Slashdot, Wired, Ain't It Cool News*, and the *New York Times*. After ilovebees.com/*The Haunted Apiary*, an ARG promoting *Halo 2*, was introduced, the game sold 2.38 million units in the first twenty-four hours in the United States and Canada, making a whopping $125 million the first day. *Perplex City* registered approximately 40,000 players between April and August and had sold about 160,000 packs of puzzle cards as of February 2006. The "extended reality" game created by Xenophile Media for the television show *ReGenesis*

Halo 2, a popular game for the Xbox video game console, was promoted, in part, by an ARG.

recently won an International Emmy at the Cannes Film Festival and generated about $2 million in revenue last year. It had more than 200,000 participants.

Right now, there are alternate reality games that are solicited by big companies, such as Microsoft or Warner Brothers, and games that are created by average people who love to play them. Some, like *The Lost Experience*, give you clues and puzzles that are merely related to a larger storyline that has been established in a TV show or movie. Others allow players to directly interact with the characters and influence the course of the story itself. Budgets range from a few thousand dollars to a few million, and the game can be as simple as taking place entirely online or as complex as organizing a game of poker in an actual cemetery.

In 2007, leading ARG experts met at ARG Fest to discuss what alternate reality gaming has done thus far and where it might be going in the future. There are so many different ways to use alternate reality gaming that people were anxious to compare notes and define it.

From the deluge of alternate reality games spreading across the net, a few separate categories have emerged.

Promotional ARGs

Probably the most well-known type of ARG is one that promotes a product. Alternate reality games have promoted everything from music albums to video games to cars.

One of the few major ARG development companies, 42 Entertainment, is primarily concerned with this type of ARG. Founded by Jordan Weisman and Elan Lee, the minds behind *The Beast*, 42 Entertainment was the driving force behind a number of ARGs—*The Haunted Apiary* (ilovebees.com), *NIN: Year Zero, Last Call Poker*, and most recently, the promotion for the upcoming Batman sequel film, *The Dark Knight*. Although the company has a Web site, it generally doesn't post much about what games it's running, so it doesn't give anything away. One of the other major ARG companies, Mind Candy, designed an ARG around the new Audi, called *The Art of the Heist*. This particular game even had participants chasing down a specific car at a rock concert to "steal" a storage card from it, which contained clues to the game.

This type of ARG is extremely popular, and the payoff is usually finding out about a highly anticipated product. For instance, fans of *The Dark Knight* got to see a preview of Heath Ledger as the Joker. Players of *The Haunted Apiary* got news of the upcoming *Halo 2* and were able to play a pre-release version of the video game upon completing the ARG.

It's a form of "viral marketing." Viral marketing is when something is so interesting people pass it on to each other or tell each other about it. The Internet is an especially great vehicle for viral marketing, since people can pass on links or information at the click of a mouse through blogging or social bookmarking sites.

ARGs can also be used to complement or accompany things that are ongoing. In between seasons two and three of the popular TV show *Lost*, there was an ARG known as *The Lost Experience*, which carried subplots of

The Art of the Heist (www.mckinney-silver.com/A3_H3ist) promoted the new Audi A3 with a fascinating ARG that ultimately had players tracking down real-life cars and retrieving information from them.

the show over the course of the summer break. For the popular TV show *ReGenesis*, Xenophile Media designed an ARG that directly incorporated characters and plots from the show through fake Web sites, e-mails, and databases that the players could access with a special password.

As alternate reality games become more prominent, skills in developing them will become extremely valuable to companies wishing to gain notoriety while marketing their product. For instance, since the *ReGenesis* ARG won an Emmy at Cannes, Xenophile Media has been busy with clients looking to do something similar.

A variety of products can be part of an ARG, including clothing. *Edoc Laundry* (www.edoclaundry.com) incorporates puzzles and storytelling into its line of trendy, stylish apparel.

Productized ARGs

Productized ARGs are similar to promotional ARGs, but instead of just promoting a product, a product is connected directly with the game itself. The most recent and popular example is the ARG *Perplex City* (designed by Mind Candy). It was free to play online but also used purchasable puzzle cards, which were themselves self-contained games. These cards were not required but they enhanced the game. Another productized ARG is *EDOC Laundry*, which is a line of quality, stylish clothing that incorporates coded puzzles and Web site URLs into the tags and graphic design, which lead curious customers

Cathy's Book

One productized ARG that really stands out is *Cathy's Book*. This young-adult novel was written by Sean Stewart and Jordan Weisman, and it is made to look like a notebook left behind by a missing girl. The book comes with a packet of other types of evidence, such as letters, phone numbers, and pictures, which are meant to lead to her whereabouts. The ARG, of course, has several related Web sites.

Sean Stewart is a science fiction author who became interested in interactive activities after being lead writer on *The Beast*. *Cathy's Book* is an interesting example of how a story can take place over a number of different mediums. What makes this ARG so interesting is that the book was written with the ARG in mind—not just as an afterthought or a promotion. The book can be read as a book or "played" as an ARG, thereby reaching a larger audience. Always try to think of different ways you can use your storytelling skills. It might just pay off.

into an ARG online. Each piece of clothing reveals a clue, and players are encouraged to share what they know online, so even people who don't buy the clothing can play the game.

Grassroots ARGs

"Grassroots" is probably a term that you'll hear a lot for different things, but in this case it refers to ARGs that are noncommercial (not paid for by a larger company) and are created by groups of ARG fans or players. Some of them, like *Orbital Colony* or *Lockjaw*, are original stories,

 Omnifam (www.omnifam.org) was an ARG that complemented the hit TV show *Alias* and eventually became intertwined with the show's plot.

being told by seasoned alternate reality gamers who are anxious to put together their own game. Other ones are based on a preexisting concept, in a similar fashion to fan fiction.

"Fan fiction" is when fans of a book, television show, movie, or game create their own stories based on it. There have been some surprisingly successful fan fiction ARGs, some of which even managed to fool people into thinking they were commercially funded. The ARG *Omnifam* was created by fans of ABC's TV show *Alias* and built on previous "official" Web games.

Grassroots ARGs are probably the most important to focus on, since successfully pulling together an alternate reality game on a limited budget is a great way to show off your skills. The point of grassroots ARGs is generally not to make money. You can't legally make money from any kind of fan fiction piece unless you have the correct permissions.

It doesn't have to cost a lot of money to tell a good story, especially if you are telling a story using the tools available on the Internet.

QUICK TIP When you watch ads on television or the Internet, consider what catches your interest and what doesn't. Humor? Honesty? Recognizable celebrities? Promotional ARGs catch people's interest in an upcoming (or existing) product by leading them down a path of puzzles or mysteries that eventually announce it.

The Cloudmakers and Brooke Thompson

From the time she was a little girl, Brooke Thompson found herself obsessed with games and puzzles. She owned an unbelievable collection of board games and integrated puzzles into everything she did—parties and artwork, among other things. She even saw the politics and social issues in the world around her as a puzzle, so she studied sociology for her undergraduate degree.

When Brooke Thompson was in college, she became intrigued by the idea of the alternate reality game for the film *A.I.* She soon became part of an ARG online community known as the Cloudmakers. The group became seasoned pros at working out clues and using member knowledge and strategy to push the story forward. When *The Beast* was finished, they had formed

 Brooke Thompson (www.mirlandano.com) has taken a love of puzzles and storytelling and turned it into a full-time career.

such close bonds as a team that they decided to put their skills to good use and design their own ARG. Thompson initially came on board as an observer, but in no time at all, she was a primary developer and played an instrumental role in the development of a brand-new independent ARG. A team of twenty-five Web designers, writers, artists, and other game enthusiasts, including Thompson, collaborated entirely online and created *Lockjaw*, which, during its run, attracted around 10,000 unique visitors to its Web site.

Thompson subsequently went back and got her master's degree in information design and technology at the Georgia Institute of Technology. She had found her passion. Brooke Thompson is now an instrumental voice in the ARG community and has a thriving career in ARG development.

She has since been a designer for *MetaCortechs*, lead designer for *Fifth Son*, as well as a variety of other roles in ARGs. Heavily intrigued by how ARGs help encourage team skills, she is also a big supporter of alternate reality gaming as an educational or training tool and has even developed the humorous training ARG *SMB: Missed Steaks.*

Xenophile Media

Xenophile Media, the company that created the ARG for *ReGenesis* and one known as *Ocular Effect* for the show *Fallen*, was started by Thomas Wallner and Patrick Crowe. They studied film at York University together and established Xenophile Media, their own new media production company, in 2001. While this may sound glamorous, the company actually started out being run from Wallner's basement. But what little exposure they did have as a company that covered digital media paid off—eventually they were approached by the producers of Shaftesbury Films with a pilot for a TV series. They were looking to have a Web site built to go with the show. Thinking they could go farther than a typical Web site, Xenophile pitched the idea of an "extended reality" game that incorporated characters and plot elements into the online experience.

Jordan Weisman

Jordan Weisman, one of the founders of 42 Entertainment, actually has a long and devoted history in the world of gaming. Growing up as a severe dyslexic, Weisman's imagination was lit up when he was introduced to the role-playing game Dungeons and Dragons, barely a year after it had been published. It encouraged him to read more, and he enjoyed not only the problem solving and the visualization but also the socialization of it. He soon became a game master himself, formed clubs, and made gaming the core of his social experience. In college, he designed and wrote his own adventures for role-playing games and sold them by tracing the gaming products he bought to their distributor and sending them samples. This way, he was able to get his work out across the country and start a business.

He focused a lot on the social aspects of gaming, even founding a company called Virtual Worlds Entertainment, which produced "Virtual Reality Centers." Before the advent of network gaming, these centers contained VR "cockpits" that were networked together to create group simulations and even had a debriefing room where players could discuss their game. The centers were not commercially successful, but it's no surprise that Weisman helped found 42 Entertainment, a company that would define a predominantly social genre of gaming.

The RPG publisher Weisman founded, Freedonia Aeronautics & Space Administration (FASA), was eventually bought by Microsoft, and Weisman was made creative director of Microsoft's entertainment division. This job, of course, was the one that brought his gaming insight to developing *The Beast* for Steven Spielberg.

As you can see, there are many ARG pros that started out just doing what they loved to do and eventually made a career out of it. At this point, there aren't going

Jordan Weisman is an influential figure in the RPG genre and is the founder of 42 Entertainment, a well-known ARG company.

to be many ARG developers that have been trained or educated specifically in alternate reality gaming. However, it takes only a little professional grounding and a keen interest in the field to make something that attracts attention. The following chapter will discuss how you can establish your place in the world of Alternate Reality Gaming.

CHAPTER THREE

USING TECHNOLOGY TO YOUR ADVANTAGE

Because alternate reality games take place in typical, everyday settings, it's not surprising that designing and developing them require a variety of skill sets, depending on the game. However, ARGs are rarely designed by just one person (as we saw with the Cloudmakers and 42 Entertainment), so you may have specific skills that can vitally enhance the game play experience of an ARG.

Teens today are surrounded by digital media: MP3 players, cell phones, and video games, as well as all of the social interaction that comes with the online universe. You probably use instant messaging or VoIP (voice over Internet protocol) as much as the phone to talk to your

Teens today rely on technology for more than just entertainment.

friends, or YouTube as much as television for entertainment. You may have tried podcasting or own an MP3 player. You've probably been familiar with some form of digital or electronic media for a significant portion of your life, so your frame of reference will be drastically different from people older than you.

You've also been around for what can only be called an explosion of social networking sites all over the Net, such as Facebook, MySpace, and Bebo. These are all sites that are bringing Internet users closer together to chat, help each other, and even participate in intellectual debate. These sites, along with more traditional forms of online groups like message boards and IRC (Internet relay chat), encourage digital communities, which are probably one of the most important factors to alternate reality gaming.

First, to really understand ARGs, you should play as many of them as possible. Whenever you play an alternate reality game, see if there is an online community of players centered around it. A good place to start would be the unFiction Forums at forums.unfiction.com, the main haunt for devoted alternate reality gamers. Learn the roles of not just the developers but also the players. Some players help keep track of all of the clues in the game so far; other players specialize in solving puzzles or interacting with characters. Learn how the players work as a team and how to take an active role in that.

According to a study by Bridge Ratings in 2007, teens between the ages of thirteen and seventeen spend an average of twelve hours a day with various types of media, including TV, radio, Internet browsing,

ALTERNATE REALITY GAMING

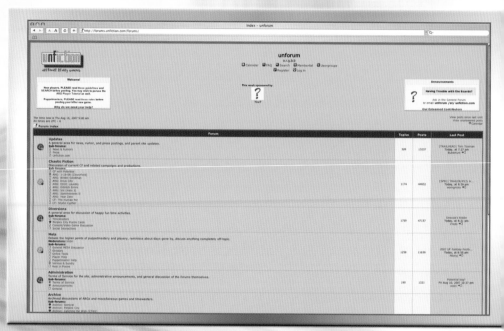

 unFiction (www.unfiction.com) is the place to trade info and puzzles solutions and to find out about the latest and greatest alternate reality games. The people you game with today may be your fellow game developers tomorrow.

MP3 players, online video, podcasting, cell phones, DVD viewing, CDs, cassettes, or e-mail. The Electronic Software Association's 2006 "Essential Facts about the Computer and Video Game Industry" reported that a little over 30 percent of the best-selling computer games in 2005 were strategy games. Not to mention, in *The Beast*, 50 percent of new players in the last six weeks were women—so it's not just guys who are playing these games.

Storytelling and Blogging

Storytelling is an essential element to alternate reality gaming. In fact, it's the backbone. But ARGs don't

Blogging is a great way to tell a story through your character's point of view. Blogger.com is a popular blogging Web site.

follow the same sort of story structure as a book or a movie—ARGs are what you would call a nonlinear form of storytelling. This means that the story will not just have a beginning, middle, and end and play straight through. It can be told out of order, but the pieces will still add up. So what are the pieces to the story? They can be online diaries, recorded phone calls, databases, Web sites, photographs, and more. You probably already have some skills to help create some of those pieces. You may also want to be one of the people who brings those pieces together (a producer), or one of the people who comes up with the story (a designer), or both.

If you like writing, practice writing in a character's "voice" through a blog. Sites like Blogger and LiveJournal offer free blog hosting, and more complicated sites like WordPress and TypePad incorporate more intensive Web design elements, which come with plenty of documentation. Blogging sites are a good place to practice Web building and coding, since some of them have templates that can be edited. WordPress offers a "pages" option for its blogs, which makes it easy to build a simple, informative Web site.

If you just want to show off your writing chops, aside from setting up a personal blog or Web site, you can submit your stories to larger sites like Associated Content or FanFiction.net. These sites are online communities with plenty of people to give feedback and suggestions for your work.

Building characters can also be as simple as setting up a free e-mail account or buying a domain name and setting up an e-mail account that way. Domain names can be purchased at a relatively low price from sites like Yahoo! and Doteasy and usually come with a small amount of hosting space.

WATCH OUT Always check "Terms of Service" agreements when you upload your work to hosting or sharing sites. Also, keep in mind that it's best not to share your phone number or address openly in your profile. Online exposure is a great way to get your work seen, but make sure that your name is tied only to works with content you feel comfortable sharing. You could even try Googling your own name periodically and see what results you get. Make sure there's nothing embarrassing!

 iPodder.com is a Web site dedicated to management of iPods. You can upload your podcasts through this site.

Experiment with Different Media

Most Apple computers now come with built-in webcams, but if you have a PC, you can buy one relatively cheaply. As well, most digital cameras now have a video capture function. You can experiment with recording short videos or films and edit them with Windows Movie Maker (a standard Windows editing program) or iMovie (the standard Macintosh video editing program). You can even use a more complicated program like Final Cut or Adobe Premiere, if you have it. There are loads of sites, like YouTube and Google, that can host your videos, which, in turn, can be "embedded" on your Web page or blog.

If you're interested in using sound, there are a number of good audio editing programs out there, such as GoldWave, but you can also do some simple audio editing using Windows Movie Maker. All you need is a microphone, and you can experiment with different audio manipulations or recordings. Practice performing in an audio file, or visit sites that have free sound effects and practice mixing them with your recording. Sites like iPodder or Podomatic allow you to upload audio files known as podcasts. You can also record

unFiction.com

The digital online community unFiction plays host to many ARG players, developers, and enthusiasts. It has everything you need to know about ARGs—terminology, history, information about the games, and things like interviews, reviews, and articles. The site even has downloadable tools to help players crack codes or solve puzzles.

Most important, there is a forum section. This is the place where players and curiosity seekers alike come to discuss and compare notes on games, or even form their own development groups. All major alternate reality games that are currently running have a thread here. The unFiction forum is a good place to check out first if you're coming into an ARG after it has already started. These threads will contain links to valuable information you'll need in order to catch up.

It's also a good place to talk about what skills you have and compare them with others to see how you can help solve a game or help develop one. There's also a live IRC (Internet relay chat).

them directly using your microphone, or in the case of gabcast.com, your cell phone. The totally free VoIP program iCall features access phone numbers and free voice mail service, if you want to incorporate phone messages into your story.

 For more complicated Web building, try Macromedia Dreamweaver or Microsoft's FrontPage Express (which might even be included in your Windows OS package). These have a user-friendly graphical interface. There are also loads of tutorials across the net, teaching you everything from CSS to JavaScript. CSS Zen Garden is a good place to find scripts that members of a Web-building community have created and shared. Making convincing and professional Web sites is important to most ARGs.

Learn from Traditional Games

ARGs don't just use digital skills. There are also a lot of other important skills to have if you're interested in designing an alternate reality game.

If you want to learn about basic game mechanics, play as many different types of games as you can. There are many different types of board games (not just Clue or Monopoly) that use different styles of game play; some are not all that different from video games. Play sports, or even games like chess, to under-stand strategy. Consider the layout of a game like Arkham Horror, and think about how it would be dif-ferent or improved as an alternate reality game . . . like chess or card games, to understand strategy.

Try different board games like Arkham Horror, which combines strategy, eerie narrative elements, and teamwork.

WATCH OUT Always remember that the "This is not a game" mandate means the suspension of disbelief, NOT hoaxing or trickery. Your work should be designed so that those reading or playing it know that it is a game. Always be prepared to explain that it is a game, should any of it result in fear, harm, or law-breaking in the real world. Also, be careful that your players and readers know the difference between what sites are involved in the game and what sites are not.

Cryptology and Puzzles

You should also become familiar with cryptology, or at least have a knowledge of a particular language or code, such as binary. Typically, clues are delivered in ARGs by way of coded messages. For instance, in the ARG *EDOC Laundry*, the codes were incorporated into the designs on the clothing itself.

Practice solving riddles and different types of puzzles to get an idea of what you can do. Look up older, traditional riddles and puzzles at your local library or buy a magazine like *GAMES*, which has a variety of clever puzzles.

Regardless of how you do it, there are plenty of online communities out there with which to collaborate on work and get feedback. Experiment and look for other people who are working at the same level as you, on the type of ARG that you're interested in. Remember that there is always a variety of literature available both online and at your local library to help you out.

CHAPTER FOUR

PLANNING YOUR EDUCATION

By now you've probably realized that teens today would consider a career that incorporates alternate reality gaming. First, you should decide which types of ARGs interest you the most. Then, try to learn as much as you can about how they work. For instance, promotional ARGs will require a slightly different approach from productized ARGs, which, in turn, will be different from ARGs used for educational purposes. From this, you can decide whether to take marketing or business courses.

Education and ARG

Take classes in the area that interests you the most—writing, design, producing, etc.—and experiment with

Taking specialized computer courses can help you explore all of the facets of computer technology and the careers available in that field.

 Math is an important part of training your brain to think in terms of puzzles —how to formulate and better understand them.

the various tools available to see what you can produce to show off your talent. If you're considering college or trying to show off your skills to a prospective employer or ARG group, a portfolio will be your best bet for showing how committed you are to learning about your category of interest. You can do small projects that show off your particular skills as an individual or try to get involved in larger collaborative projects, much like the Cloudmakers did.

Plan your high school and college courses accordingly, if you can. Take English to understand story archetypes and classic literature. This will also improve your critical thinking skills. Learning another language

ARGFest-o-Con

Although this relatively new genre of gaming is only a few years old, there is already a conference being organized around it. In March 2007, the important names in alternate reality gaming gathered in San Francisco to explain, define, speculate, consider, and debate alternate reality gaming. Industry leaders such as Dave Szulborski, Brooke Thompson, and Evan Jones sat in on panels to discuss a number of topics related to ARGs: how to develop an ARG, how to run an ARG, and what the future holds for the genre.

Conventions and trade shows are extremely important. It's a good chance to get to know other professionals in the industry and hear what they have to say in real time. You can also actively participate in discussions and make useful contacts with other aspiring developers.

Outside of that, they can also be a great place to meet people and socialize. People come from all over the place to attend conferences and trade shows, so you never know who you're going to meet!

Even if you can't make it to a convention or conference, Google it to see if you can find uploaded videos or podcast recordings of panels. That way you can at least get a taste of what you missed.

may also be helpful. Math can help you formulate puzzles and better understand how a game works. In speaking with Brooke Thompson, she told us, "Math is pretty important, and you use it more than you think you would—games are, in many ways, math problems filled with odds and statistics. It's not something that you think about while you're doing it, so it's important to have a basic understanding of it that you can draw on without thinking."

Obviously, any courses that teach Web design would be useful, both in learning the visual layout of a Web page and learning to code the various elements of it by hand and with a visual interface, such as Dreamweaver.

Extracurricular Activities and ARG

Don't just look at classes—extracurricular activities can also be invaluable. Brooke Thompson recommended joining a theater group. "Whether you are acting, working on props, or doing the sound and lighting," she said, "you will learn what it is like to be a part of a production. That's something that is very difficult to get out of a book and is incredibly valuable to an ARG team."

Also, try joining a role-playing club, if your school has one. Apart from learning to think and speak as a fictional character in real time, you'll also get experience handling the players if you organize a game yourself. Writing a role-playing module is easy enough, but it takes skill to plan for the unpredictability of those playing the game.

Join a sports team to reinforce teamwork and game play. Join a debate team to practice critical thinking. There are a number of ways you can intellectually prepare yourself for ARG design and development.

The movies can teach you a lot about how to use a visual medium in different ways, and DVDs often have extra content that can educate viewers about the production process.

 Drama not only helps you learn to play a part but also how to work with a group of people (a production team) to visualize and create a story.

Consider college or university programs like marketing, sociology, or psychology to understand the audience of your stories.

One field that would be incredibly useful to study would be new media or interactive media. Quite a few colleges and universities across the country have programs where you can study how media and technology are changing our lives and how we interact with each other. These programs teach you how to think out of the box and how to consider ways in which we can put technologies to good use in entertainment and education.

Take in as much media as you can—books, films, newspapers, television (yes, even television), video

 You can post photos and bits of your visual art on an online photo community like Flickr (www.flickr.com).

games, and online media, too. Eventually you'll start to notice the differences between them and how that matters when it comes to telling a story.

Identifying Skills for ARG

To understand and enjoy working with ARGs, you have to have a knowledge of the Internet. How to use search engines, how HTML works, and how to find different types of information are all important. Ultimately, your audience will largely include tech-savvy people who know how to sniff out a code or look at the source code of a Web page. You also have to know how to find emerging Internet technology and use it to your advantage. For instance, maybe one of your characters will have a blog or a social networking profile on something like MySpace or Facebook. Maybe players will need to contact a character via Skype or MSN Messenger. Perhaps they have a photo gallery on Flickr that will give your players valuable clues that pertain to the story.

But more than that, you should also have knowledge on a broad range of subjects. Why? Because collectively, so will the people playing. This doesn't mean you have to know everything! Even if you have an obscure hobby or a knowledge of classic literature, you can integrate these things to add extra dimension to your story.

CHAPTER FIVE

PRESENTING, PRESERVING, AND SHOWING YOUR WORK

Before you even begin applying to colleges, you can showcase your work all in one place by creating a portfolio Web site. Not only will you have a self-contained link to give to fellow developers and employers, but it's also a good chance to practice your skills in design, coding, or writing, since building a Web site often requires all three. It doesn't have to be complex or fancy. It should be clean and professional looking, with easy navigation.

Keep it clear of too much personal material like online diaries or photo albums. Because it's the Web, you can make a resume in HTML that hyperlinks to examples of your work. Hyperlinking can also be done in Microsoft Word.

Doteasy.com is one site where you can purchase hosting space for your own Web site.

Domain names are relatively cheap and can easily be registered. Keep in mind that domain names don't always come with hosting space to store the pages and images, so make sure that you don't have a Web site with large video and picture files. Try to "optimize" your images for the Web, and keep audio and video in more compressed formats such as MP3 or MPEG, or host them on a separate site. Doteasy gives you a small amount of hosting space when you register a domain, and sites like YouTube and Photobucket are good for hosting media, as

The SXSW Interactive Festival

South by Southwest (SXSW) caters to filmmakers, musicians, and most important, those involved in the field of interactive media. There are a few different festivals running for SXSWeek, but the one you should primarily be concerned with is the Interactive Festival. The Interactive Festival is "ground zero for the world's most creative Web developers, designers, bloggers, wireless innovators, and new media entrepreneurs." The festival includes panels, presentations, and a three-day trade show and exhibition. It also now has Screenburn programming geared specifically toward the gaming industry and a two-day arcade.

The 2007 Interactive Festival took place in March in Austin, Texas. A number of industry leaders attended, and there was even a section for alternate reality gaming.

they have unlimited space and bandwidth and can be pasted directly into a Web page. (Bandwidth represents how much your media is being accessed or downloaded.)

In terms of packaging your work for showing to people offline, interactive pieces can be burned to a CD. Make sure that files are in a typical format that most computers can read, like MS Word, Flash, MPEG, or MP3, and that they are complete and relatively self-contained. Always bring a hard-copy version of noninteractive elements of your portfolio, like your resume, articles, pictures, and screenshots just in case. Put it together in a binder or folder with transparency sheets so that you don't lose anything.

For a college or job interview, make sure you are dressed cleanly and professionally. Keep in mind that every interview is different, and you should do your research well in advance.

There's no denying that it's fun to be a cyber sleuth, but alternate reality gaming also builds team skills. When participants on a message board work together, it's surprising the number of different skills and experience that can be put to use. In *The Beast*, the skills of the Cloudmakers ranged from complex decoding to something as obscure as understanding the tablature of a lute.

Job Positions Within the ARG Field

Like a theater production, each person in a development team has a role to play—from the complex puzzles to the voice on the end of the telephone. The designers are the people that conceptualize the structure and design of the game itself. The producer is the person

 Confidence, professionalism, and a killer portfolio can do wonders during a pivotal college or job interview.

that helps pull all the pieces together by organizing the budget, finding the right people for the right job, and generally just figuring out how it can all be done. These things require good people skills and an ability to budget. Graphic designers help visualize the story and give it its look and feel. And writers assist in telling the story and give the characters their personalities.

Depending on the ARG, there will be a variety of shoes to fill, but those are the most important ones. On most ARG development teams, people will be doing more than one job, so it helps to have a variety of skills and knowledge. Everybody on a team should understand and respect everyone else's job so that it's easy to work as a team and make sure everything gets done. Often, these development teams (especially the grassroots ones) do not meet in real life, but online. When a team is collaborating digitally, each member needs to have a strong commitment to the project and a great deal of self-discipline. These skills not only apply to alternate reality gaming but also to a variety of other types of jobs and careers that you may get into.

Small Projects and Networking

Employers and colleges aren't just looking for "hard skills" like writing or art. They're also looking for "soft skills"—leadership, teamwork, organization, self-discipline, and the ability to work under a deadline. They're not just looking for past jobs or school grades but also smaller projects that show initiative you've taken on your own.

Social networking sites like myspace.com and facebook.com are great places to meet people with similar tastes and hobbies—and possibly even post some of your work.

The best way to do this is to network. You can do this online by joining a Web community like unFiction or social networking sites like Facebook or MySpace. (Remember to keep it professional looking!) You can also try meeting people in person. Look for trade shows, conventions, or social events related to alternate reality games. The genre is new, but there are already a few of them running in places around the country, and other types of trade shows, like the Game Developer's Conference, have incorporated sections for alternate reality gaming as well. You can also visit IGDA.org (International Game Developers Association) and find out the closest chapter to you and where and when it meets. Despite the fact that video games and ARGs are only "cousins," they share enough qualities of interactive storytelling that they are still an important topic to IGDA.

Most chapters of IGDA hold monthly social nights or events for members to get together. Dress clean and semi-casually and be prepared to talk to both industry professionals and ambitious students about what you know and what you'd like to know. Even contacts that you make now, with people at the same level as you, may come in handy in the future. Remember that how you present yourself will go a long way toward making a good impression; don't be rude or obnoxious, otherwise someone important could remember you for the wrong reasons! When you do have an opinion to offer, offer it in a constructive and intelligent manner.

Most important of all, show that you're passionate about alternate reality gaming and that you've done your homework. It always pays off to be serious about

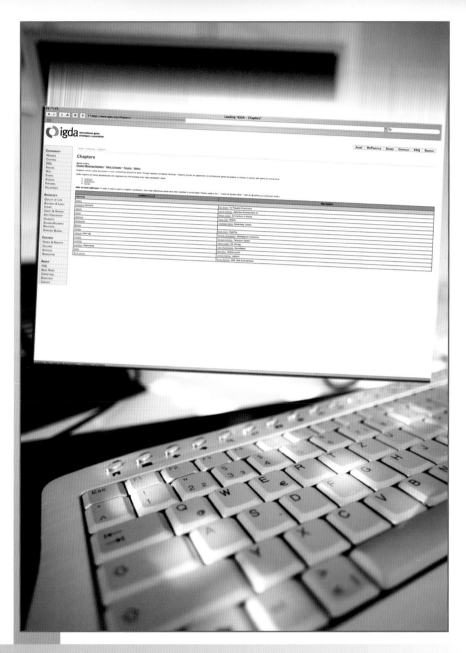

Keep active in your local IGDA chapter by attending its meetings and social events. You could meet someone important in the industry.

anything that you do. That way, eventually you can put your skills to good use. By taking the time to read this book, you are already well on your way to finding a career in the field of Alternate Reality Gaming. Good luck!

GLOSSARY

blog Short for "Web log." This term now covers not only online journals, but also sites that provide daily news or updates on various topics.

fan fiction A story or work that borrows characters or a fictional world from somebody else's intellectual property, usually without permission. Fans write fan fiction in tribute to what they love (books, movies, TV shows, etc.) with no intent to sell it or claim it as their own.

intellectual property Music, stories, movies, art, etc., constitute intellectual property. These are things that were created by somebody.

IRC (Internet relay chat) This is a large network of Internet chat channels or rooms used on a number of Web sites and chat clients.

podcast A longer MP3 recording that can be posted and downloaded for a person to listen to on his or her MP3 player. Usually, podcasts are online radio shows, but like blogging, they can be a variety of other things.

puppet masters This term refers to the development team of an ARG and the fact that they are never seen or heard from directly during the course of the game. They're out of the way and pulling the strings instead.

rabbit hole The entry point into an alternate reality game. This term is inspired by Lewis Carroll's *Alice in Wonderland* and sums up the passive way in which most ARGs start. Whether it's an odd phrase on a movie poster or a URL at the end of a trailer, the rabbit hole is generally a seemingly innocent reference that leads the player straight into the game.

social networking sites Sites, like MySpace, Facebook, Bebo, or hi5, that let you post information about yourself and connect with people around the world that have similar tastes. You can send messages, form groups, and post photos. MySpace has the added bonus of allowing musical artists to post their latest tracks.

viral marketing What happens when a product or news bite comes along that is so interesting or funny that people want to pass it along. For instance, YouTube is a great place to find videos that have "gone viral" because it's easy to pass on links.

VoIP (Voice over Internet protocol) VoIP is chatting vocally across the Internet, either through an instant messenger or VoIP program. This can be done either with headphones and a microphone headset or a specialized VoIP phone that plugs into your computer. Some VoIP subscriptions can connect to landline phones.

FOR MORE INFORMATION

Alternate Reality Gaming Network
Box 311
La Broquerie, MB R0A 0W0
Canada
Web site: http://www.argn.com
An online news resource for alternate reality gaming
  enthusiasts and professionals.

Association for Applied Interactive Multimedia
P.O. Box 182
Charleston, SC 29402-0182
Web site: http://aaim.org
An association that provides resourceful materials for
  professionals who work in the field of interactive
  multimedia.

Entertainment Software Association
575 7th Street NW, Suite 300
Washington, DC 20004
Web site: http://www.theesa.com
E-mail: esa@theesa.com
An association that works to provide resources for
  companies that publish video games.

International Game Developers Association
870 Market Street, Suite 1181
San Francisco, CA 94102-3002

(415) 738-2104
Web site: http://info@igda.org
An organization that helps game developers connect
  with each other and advance within their field.

unFiction, Inc.
941 NW Naito Pkwy #315
Portland, OR 97209
Web site: http://www.unfiction.com
A resource and forum for people interested in alternate
  reality gaming.

Web Sites

Due to the changing nature of Internet links, Rosen
Publishing has developed an online list of Web sites related
to the subject of this book. This site updated regularly.
Please use this link to access the list:

http://www.rosenlinks.com/dcb/arga

FOR FURTHER READING

Crawford, Chris. *Chris Crawford on Game Design.* Berkeley, CA: New Riders Games, 2003.

Crawford, Chris. *Chris Crawford on Interactive Storytelling.* Berkeley, CA: New Riders Games, 2004.

Fowles, John. *The Magus*, rev. ed. New York, NY: Back Bay Books, 2001.

Gibson, William. *Pattern Recognition.* New York, NY: Berkley, 2005.

Gosney, John W. *Beyond Reality: A Guide to Alternate Reality Gaming.* Boston, MA: Course Technology PTR, 2005.

Salen, Katie, and Eric Zimmerman. *Rules of Play: Game Design Fundamentals.* Cambridge, MA: The MIT Press, 2003.

Stewart, Sean. *Cathy's Book: If Found Call 650-266-8233.* Philadelphia, PA: Running Press Kids, 2006.

Szulborski, Dave. *This Is Not a Game: A Guide to Alternate Reality Gaming.* Morrisville, NC: Lulu.com, 2005.

Van Delft, Pieter. *Creative Puzzles of the World.* New York, NY: H. N. Abrams, 1978.

BIBLIOGRAPHY

Dena, Christy. "Top ARGs with Stats." Cross Media
    Entertainment. March 2006. Retrieved May 2007
    (http://www.crossmediaentertainment.com).

Electronic Software Association. "Essential Facts About
    the Computer and Video Game Industry." 2006.
    Retrieved June 2007 (http://www.theesa.com/files/
    2005EssentialFacts.pdf).

eMarketer. "Generation Y Multitaskers Boost Media
    Time." June 21, 2007. Retrieved June 2007 (http://
    www.emarketer.com).

Martin, Adam, ed. "2006 Alternate Reality Games
    Whitepaper: IGDA Alternate Reality Games SIG."
    International Game Developers Association. 2006.
    Retrieved April 2007 (http://igda.org/arg).

Rojas, Peter. "A Conspiracy of Conspiracy Gamers."
    Wired. September 19, 2001. Retrieved May 2007
    (http://www.wired.com/culture/lifestyle/news/
    2001/09/46672).

SXSW Interactive Conference. "ARG! The Attack of the
    Alternate Reality Games Panel." March 2007.
    Retrieved May 2007 (http://danhon.com/2007/05/
    23/sxsw-2007-arg-the-attack-of-the-alternate-reality-
    games-transcript).

Thompson, Brooke. "Biography." Retrieved May 2007 (http://www.mirlandano.com/biography/index.html).

Thompson, Brooke. Interview with author. June 2007.

Wikipedia. "Alternate Reality Game." Retrieved April 2007 (http://en.wikipedia.org/wiki/Alternate_reality_game).

Wong, Tony. "Interactive with an X." *Toronto Star*. June 18, 2007. Retrieved June 2007 (http://www.thestar.com/Business/article/226419)

INDEX

About the Author

Meg Swaine has a diploma in online writing and information design from Centennial College and a bachelor's degree in creative writing from York University. Through the online writing program, she developed an interest in new media and interactive storytelling. She has since spent much time writing within and about the online community. She authored a previous title in this series, *Career Building Through Interactive Online Games*.

Photo Credits

Cover, pp. 1, 28 Shutterstock.com; p. 5 © Matthew Peyton/ Getty Images; p. 8 © William Thomas Cain/Getty Images; p. 10 © AP Images; p. 12 © Everett Collection; p. 15 © Chris Hondros/Getty Images; p. 26 © PR Newswire Photo Service/Newscom; p. 36 Wikipedia; p. 38 © James Marshall/ The Image Works; p. 39 © www.istockphotos.com/ Krystyna Trojanowska; p. 42 © Erik Dreyer/Stone/Getty Images; pp. 43, 49 (top) © Bob Daemmrich/The Image Works; p. 49 (bottom) © www.istockphoto.com/Jamie Duplass; p. 53 (background) © www.istockphoto.com/ Alexander Hafemann.

Designer: Nelson Sá; **Editor:** Bethany Bryan
Photo Researcher: Amy Feinberg